The Animals' Refuge
A Centenary History of the National Equine Defence League

Celebrating one hundred years of
caring for animals

By

Jackie Moffat

Published by the Animals' Refuge,
Oak Tree Farm, Wetheral Shields, Carlisle, Cumbria

www. animalrefuge.co.uk

Published 2009

Printed by Finger prints, Barrow-in-Furness

ISBN 978-0-9562648-0-0

FOREWORD BY KATIE MORAG

I was a foundling. I'm not sure where, exactly, I was foundled but from there, I was brought to the Animals' Refuge and given a tag: Dog 151. The folk there fed me, gave me water, took me for walks and paid me a great deal of attention. I quickly became aware that I was a very important dog indeed.

In time, some of my neighbours moved on, and so, I learned, would I. But where would I go? Could I choose? I had a word with t'Boss here, telling him, in no uncertain terms – me being a very important dog and all that – to find me some nice humans, with time and space and love to give me.

One day, a couple came and seemed to rather take to me. They looked – and I'd be grateful if you'd keep this to yourself – a right pair of suckers. So I wagged my tail rather more than usual, and pricked my ears. But they went away. They came back though, a day or so later, with Tess, an elderly collie. She had big brown eyes, a silky coat and obviously a pretty cushy life. Her sister had died and she was lonely so she interviewed me for the vacancy of Lady's Companion, and we shook on the deal – well, we would have done if we'd had hands, not paws, which aren't all that great for shaking. She promised plenty of Bonios, long walks, our own fields, a chair or two – all I had to do to gain access to this doggy Nirvana was to obey her rules. Fair enoughski.

We got along just fine. As far as I could gather, the only day's work she had ever done was a modelling job: her human needed a Cover Girl for a book. I could do that, I thought, and of course, in the fullness of time, I did. I was so good at it, I've done it again, for this history. Sometimes, my humans ask me "Who were you before you were Katie Morag?" But the past, as some wise human once said, is another country. For some of us here, it's another planet, thank heaven. I know I was Dog 151 at the Refuge, but as for the bit before that, do you know, I can hardly remember. Perhaps I would just rather forget.

This is my story, and there are many, many others like it from the Refuge: dogs, cats, ferrets, rabbits, birds, goats, donkeys, and ponies, too, of course, because it was the pit ponies at the turn of the last century that started the whole thing off. We all want our own special home, and many of us find it, but those that don't stay as long-term residents.

We all have reason to be grateful to Francis Cox and everyone who has continued his work. Without him, and his successors, my story, and theirs, would be very, very different.

Katie Morag, Lurcher Extraordinaire

THE NATIONAL EQUINE & SMALLER ANIMALS DEFENCE LEAGUE

1909

The National Equine Defence League was founded by Francis Cox, whose primary aim was to improve the lives and working conditions of the 71,000 pit ponies working in Britain's mines. The first meeting of the League was held in London and presided over by Jerome K Jerome.

And elsewhere in 1909:

Woolworths, too was founded

Selfridges 'brought American style to London'

Bakelite, the ubiquitous substance that graced homes during the first half of the twentieth century in the form of radios and telephones was invented

Niagara falls froze

Bleriot flew the Channel in 43 minutes, claiming a £1000 prize offered by the Daily Mail. And £1000 was a fortune in 1909…

Henry Ford advertised his Model T, with the memorable slogan "any colour you like as long as it's black."

Crystal Palace Football Club lost its appeal against a claim for compensation for match injuries by one of its players. Why? The Club's assertion that the footballer was 'playing a game' rather than working, was thrown out, his lawyer successfully claiming that the player had 'surrendered to the club the bodily labour of his arms and legs and that he was a servant, in that he had to obey the Club's orders.' Who said compo was new?

The keel of the Titanic was laid.

A little history

The Early Years: foundation and establishment of The National Equine Defence League

"Oh, let him go. He has made as much as will buy another or two like him."

"Never mind. What kills one buys another."

Extracts from two letters from colliers

It was attitudes like these that impelled Francis Cox to found the National Equine Defence League, as it was properly known at its inception in 1909. Cox embarked, initially, on a one-man crusade, seeking to improve conditions for pit ponies that lived, worked, were injured and often died, in appalling conditions. Poorly managed, inadequately rested, inhumanely treated and cast aside when they foundered, a pit pony could expect no compassion throughout a working life of abject misery and as there were something like 71,000 ponies working down the pits in 1909, it was a concern of epic proportions.

Others quickly rallied round Francis Cox. Keir Hardie, who had worked as a pony driver in the mines in Scotland, and was later to found the modern Labour Party, wrote to Cox:

"I … look back with a feeling of shame on some of the scenes I witnessed."

Jerome K Jerome – yes, the very same man who wrote the hilarious Three Men in a Boat – presided at the inaugural meeting of the League, on 9 June 1909 and spoke of "cruelty, grim and appalling does exist to this day in literally the dark places of the earth." It was hard to imagine a starker evocation of misery.

At that meeting, a resolution was passed:
"That an organisation, to be called the National Equine Defence League be founded to establish and maintain the humane usage and proper treatment of horses and donkeys, by the means of an education programme which shall enlighten the persons in charge of such animals as to their natural capacities and instincts and thereby ensure the natural and habitual exercise of mercy."

It wasn't a huge thing to ask, really, given the vital work the animals performed, daily and without respite.

So it was that the League determined to *"concentrate all its energies and abilities specifically to the reform of the present conditions and treatment of pit ponies and devote itself solely to that end until it is accomplished."*

There was no messing about. By the 4 July, the League had laid the facts before the Home Secretary and by August 1909, a pamphlet – a popular way of disseminating information in the days before radio and television - The Legal Status of the Pit Pony was published. By October, the government had agreed to an investigation and in 1910, the newly appointed Home Secretary, one Winston Churchill took up the matter, with his trademark terrier-like tenacity and bullishness – how strange that the most obvious terms to apply to Churchill both draw comparisons between the great man and animal characteristics!

Cox's public awareness campaign inspired articles in the popular press, notably in the February 1910 issue of The Animals' Advocate, a magazine devoted to the interests of all animals, where colourful headlines included *Alleged cruelty to Wolves; Cats Roasted Alive; Horrible Plight of a Sheep* and *Vicarage Servant Roasts Cat*. Aside from the unhealthy amount of cat-roasting going on, the magazine gave vocal support to the League. It seems reasonable to surmise that pit pony welfare, or lack of it, was now a matter of popular debate, and that many people had a view on it.

Largely as a result of Churchill's Royal Commission, the 1911 Coal Mines Act came into force in July 1912 and contained a total of six clauses specifically relating to pit pony welfare. For the first time, the pit pony was protected by statute and in December 1912, the League recorded "hearty thanks to Mr Winston Churchill for the appointment of the Royal Commission and the inclusion of the consideration of the horses' treatment in the scope of the Mines Bill..."

But Cox, acutely aware that passing legislation and enforcing it were two rather different things, had a lively exchange of correspondence with Gladstone, pressing consistently for further improvement. Inspections eventually became mandatory – although Cox lamented that the number of inspectors was absurdly inadequate - but it was, at least, a start. Jerome K Jerome waded in with a fierce letter in the Press, and Cox himself produced a pamphlet, The Tragedy of the Pit Pony, citing practices barbaric beyond imagining:

" (in) *collieries where cages are not large enough to receive the horses, their legs were tied together and the animal placed in a strong net and lowered down into the pit by a winch...*"

Kicking, beating and overwork of the animals, Cox reported to be commonplace.

Whilst the League continued campaigning for the pit ponies, it also turned its attention to other equine welfare issues. Docking – the hideous practice of chopping off a horse's tail in the erroneous belief that a full tail somehow affected its efficiency in harness - was vigorously opposed. Indeed, it was Jack London, writer of the celebrated book, *Call of the Wild*, who produced the campaigning pamphlet for the League on this issue. Interestingly, hunting folk had already abandoned docking.

The harness horse – and it's worth remembering that in the first decade of the twentieth century, the horse was the primary means of transport, either ridden or driven - was the focus of another of the League's campaigns. Strenuous efforts were made to persuade drivers to slacken bearing reins and hame reins. Talk to anyone who knows anything about the technicalities of carriage driving and they will tell you that the horse does not **pull** a carriage; instead, he **pushes** into his collar, and it is that pushing which powers the vehicle's progress. The League wrote to the King, complaining that the bearing reins on royal horses were far too tight, and to General Bramwell Booth in similar vein, about the animals so impeded at his late father's funeral. Booth's response was sympathetic, incidentally, but records sadly fail to elicit details of the King's reaction.

The League erected signs imploring drivers to slacken the bearing and hame reins at significant locations, among which were Kingston Hill in Surrey – and anyone who has cycled up Kingston Hill will attest to its steepness – Sutton Bank – ever followed a tractor up there? – and Heath Street in leafy Hampstead. It is a shame that none of these signs remain in situ, but a picture is reproduced amongst our illustrations.

As early as 1913 the League had a stand at the Royal Agricultural Show at Bristol, very much in the spirit of public education, and also concerned itself with the welfare of seaside donkeys and performing animals. A century on, very few animals 'perform' at circuses and the like, but back in the early twentieth century, this was popular.

By 1914, the League was starting to embrace the needs of canines as well as equines, although the fate of horses used in the First World War was one of the League's primary preoccupations at this time. "Patching up" horses injured in battle was labelled "a disgrace", and the callous abandonment of cast-offs sold to casual purchasers – not so dissimilar to the fate of many a cast-off racehorse in the modern world – castigated.

Contributors to the magazine *The New Age* in 1916 included Hilaire Belloc, holding forth on *The Coming of Servile Labour;* elsewhere in the same publication, amongst other robust views and opinions, a letter from Francis Cox expressed disgust at the Army's indifference to horses – and indeed, their owners – who had become involved in this aspect of the War. Cox cited the experience of a lady farmer, and subscriber to the League, as follows:

At the beginning of the War, we received from a lady farmer, one of our subscribers, a most pathetic letter. At that time of national emergency she did not demur to her horses being commandeered for Army service; but in view of the fact that they were not only agricultural horses, but domestic pets, practically part of her household, and from their earliest days had been treated as such, she urgently requested us to do what we could to ensure their return to her after the war, if they survived. Only an animal lover can realise her feelings and anxiety on the matter and surely an accession to such a request was the smallest possible recognition of the greatness of her personal sacrifice. We immediately laid the matter before the War Office and received the usual stereotyped reply that nothing could be done. Why, it is impossible to conceive, because, from enquiries

I then and have since made I have found that all horses used by the Army are identified by marks and registered and surely it would have involved but an inappreciable amount of work to return them to their original owners. This callous general abandonment of Army horses to fates which in most cases are terrible to surmise is bad enough; but the reckless indifference displayed in flinging animals whose senses and instincts have been trained up to almost human aptitude to any casual unknown purchaser is nothing more nor less than a scandal and an atrocity disgraceful to us as a nation."

Vigorous campaigns were waged against the "Decrepit Horse Traffic" – animals whose working lives were over, but were callously sold for meat. And that, too, remains a concern a hundred years on: live horses are still transported in some pretty dire conditions to satisfy the continental palate for horse-meat. Some things, sadly, do not change.

The extraordinary Francis Cox died in 1920. Fittingly, a drinking trough memorial was erected in Bowes Road, Southgate, London to his memory, inscribed

In Memory of Francis Cox
(The Pit Pony's Friend)
He lived and died to help the helpless, to plead the cause of those
who hunger and thirst, toil and suffer in silence
1862-1920

The Flappers' Years to the Forties

Throughout the twenties, while flappers danced in fashionable low-waisted dresses and smoked cigarettes from long holders, the League beavered away, drawing attention to the overweighting of two-year old racehorses on the tracks, and the overloading of working animals on slippery roads. With commendable prescience, the League also worked to abolish vivisection – a cause that became much more high-profile in the 1960's and 1970's – and continued to rail against docking and the decrepit horse trade.

The League's 1929 Report records some events of quite incredible cruelty and callousness:

- A three-legged colt found in a sideshow at the Olympia Circus in London
- A pony whose fetlocks and hooves had been tortured to give the appearance of a camel when on stage; a false hump had been stuck on its back. The pony was sent from the South of England and shipped from Liverpool to Dublin in a crate, condemned to stand in one position all the time. The unfortunate animal was bought by the League and shot. This pony's picture tells its own story, and fully explains the League's determination to bring an end to this trade.

A number of ponies, listed in the 1929 report, had been rescued by the League and either given a short time of freedom and rest before a humane death, or subject to "rigid agreement" that they would not pass out of the League's care. Numerous prosecutions for cruelty are also listed, and make for fairly unedifying reading.

The pit ponies' plight was still a very hot topic. Of the 50,405 ponies employed below ground, nearly two thousand died or had to be destroyed because of injury or accident. Another 1,720 died from disease. Over five thousand cases of injury were reported to management and a further 75 due to ill-treatment. These are shocking statistics by any standards.

Meanwhile, in 1925, and near to the League's current home, Alfred Brisco formed the Carlisle Animals' Friend Society. Greatly worried by the heartless methods employed to destroy unwanted animals – weighted sacks in rivers being reportedly used to drown dogs and cats – Mr Brisco established a clinic where humane destruction could be carried out and travelled the area in his motor bike and sidecar, operating a one-man euthanasia service. The archives reveal a charming euphemism for this: sick dogs "were slept away in their homes…" A veterinary service, too, followed.

Alfred Brisco was born in 1897, son of John and Sarah Brisco, well known Carlisle basket-makers. He worked as a nurseryman on leaving school, until the start of the First World War when he joined the Tank Corps, where he became a tank driver; his personal memoir of the Battle of Cambria, written in unemotional, level prose reveals a man of extraordinary fortitude and bravery. He recalls "Personally I did not see the cavalry in action at all. The one major thing the Cambria Battle did was to show how cavalry could be effectively substituted by armoured mechanisation." This did not stop him feeling "a great compassion for these wretched animals. So when I left the army I often thought of them and I greatly desired in some way to work for the welfare of all animals and birds which I learned were in many ways most shamefully exploited." It was hardly surprising, given what Alfred Brisco had witnessed during wartime, that painless euthanasia of suffering animals should be his highest priority: he knew, and understood, that sometimes, keeping an animal alive was neither right nor realistic.

Alfred Brisco dedicated his life to improving the lot of animals; there is even a suggestion that at one stage, he travelled to France in disguise and virtually undercover to research the force-feeding of geese to produce foie gras, a practice that would undoubtedly have been anathema to him. As well as his Carlisle Animals' Friend Society, he later travelled widely on another one-man mission to educate the public about animal welfare, campaigning across Britain and on the continent, for the introduction of proper welfare regulations surrounding the humane slaughter of meat animals. That such regulations were eventually enacted and enforced, was due in no small part to his tireless efforts. Predictably, he himself became a lifelong vegetarian, a vigorous opponent of blood sports and vivisection, and a vociferous campaigner against the export of poor quality or worn out horses and ponies. In time, legislation ensured that only animals over a certain value were granted an export licence, this Minimum Value ending the misery of live exports of poor quality or unfit equines. Many years later, his efforts to ban the use of cruel 'gin traps' also bore fruit, these inhumane traps that often wounded and led to a slow and grisly death for the animal caught, rather than killing them outright, being outlawed, although at first only in England and Wales. The law amending the legislation to include Scotland finally went through in 1972, a few weeks after Alfred Brisco's death.

In the 1930's, and in collaboration with Alfred Brisco, the National Equine Defence League established a Home of Rest for Horses in Carlisle, with Alfred appointed its Director and as time passed, the League's activities took on another dimension, supporting other animal welfare organisations. Reflecting the gradual merger of Brisco's clinic and the Home of Rest for Horses, the League's name was amended to The National Equine (and Smaller Animals) Defence League, and that nomenclature remains to this day. The recognition that some animals could not be cured or rehabilitated was significant, and the League took the stance that such animals should be put out of their misery as quickly and painlessly as possible; many others were rescued, including a white horse Tommy – "a most remarkable animal, 36 years old", Lassie, who was received into the home in a very nervous condition with a sore back but who completely recovered after two months care, and Old Tom, in Alfred Brisco's own words "an old white army horse" he came upon at Brough Hill Fair, where he was "being shamefully knocked about." After two months peaceful rest, though, Old Tom had to be humanely destroyed.

Another extraordinary man was now at the helm, following in the noble tradition of Francis Cox.

The War Years and Beyond

Up until this time, the League was based in London, with offices in Victoria Street, along a bit from the Albert pub and almost opposite where Pizza Express is now. How times change. With the outbreak of World War Two in 1939, the Executive Council decided it would be expedient to relocate the League's Head Office and centre of administration to the Carlisle operation; there was every intention of moving back to the capital once the War was over, but experience during those years taught that firstly, substantial savings could be made by being less London-centric, and secondly, that the League could pursue its various campaigns just as effectively from the Cumbrian countryside. So, the move back to the capital never came to pass, and the League remains in Cumbria, although no longer at Blackwell near Carlisle, as it was then, but at Oak Tree Farm, of which, more later. Air raids in London meant that the Rest Fields at New Southgate in London had to be abandoned and the horses moved; the land was let to Friern Barnet Urban District Council for allotments.

A snapshot of the League's work in 1940, makes for interesting reading. The Animals Guardians, a Junior Section of the League was established, in the spirit of "catch 'em young" and by June 1942, the Animals' Guardians numbered 6500. Smaller animal work expanded, rest and rehabilitation of working horses continued, the League had a presence at auction marts, actively tried to educate owners of animals of all sorts as to their care and welfare, particularly their farriery and feeding, liased with other charities in the same field, and campaigned against hunting. Depressingly, docking still remained legal, though the League remained as implacably opposed to it and as determined to see it outlawed as ever.

The office diary of the time made passing mention too of events beyond the League's boundaries: "Aug 15 1945 – War with Japan ceased last night at midnight. Mary is at Pontefract ... Phloxes still going strong – must plan for next year, somewhat as follows: Primulas and wallflowers ..."

The annual reports chronicling the war years are unsurprisingly thin volumes, but with 1946, came renewed activity in many spheres of the League's concerns. Officers and Inspectors attended sales fairs and slaughterhouses, the call to withdraw ponies from the pits altogether gained momentum and the League acquired a "New Motor Van" to collect injured and stray animals in the Tyneside area.

Campaigning, rehabilitation of all types of animals continued unabated and by the late fifties, the League had added the strapline "Objects: to protect all animals, domesticated and wild" to its annual report. The post-war years also saw the emphasis of the League's activities move away from a primarily campaigning stance, and towards a more hands-on approach. Much had been achieved for the pit ponies and indeed for other equines, but the importance of the horse as a vital cog in society's transport wheels was diminishing rapidly by now, as motorised transport increased.

In 1964, Frank Tebbutt became the General Secretary of the League, with special responsibility for developing the League's work for smaller animals. Alfred Brisco continued as Director and of course, with his extensive propaganda work as well as having specific responsibility for the larger animals, particularly pit ponies. Posters promoting animal welfare and opposing bull-fighting were now being sent abroad by the League, which had now stepped back from its original position, no longer calling for the immediate withdrawal of ponies from the pits, Alfred Brisco having elected to compromise on this, saying that ponies should gradually be replaced by mechanical haulage systems and until that time, the League would provide the ponies that came out of the mines wit "a good spell of retirement in our Homes of Rest"

The death of Sir Winston Churchill was marked by a touching notice in the 1964 Report, no doubt worded by Alfred Brisco:

Sir Winston Churchill

With the Passing to the Higher Life of this great Spirit, we do not forget the full part he played in 1911 in the appointment of the Royal Commission, and the inclusion of the consideration of the ponies treatment in the scope of the Mines Bill, the first protection the pit ponies had on Statue.
We will not add our RIP became we could not imagine him "resting." His "job" will be prepared ready for him.

Away back in 1908 he said:
"What is the use of living if it be not to strive for noble Causes and to make this muddled world a better place for those who will live in it after we are gone."
He played his full part in "this muddled world" and his live will ever be an inspiration.

Alfred Brisco himself died in 1972, as already mentioned, and in March 1972 Frank Tebbutt was appointed Organising Secretary of the League, whose work had now expanded to the point where new premises were needed.

An appeal was launched. Amongst the high profile supporters who lent their weight to this drive for funds were the celebrated climber Sir Chris Bonnington, the Bishop of Carlisle and the Mayor of

Carlisle. Half the money needed was raised, and Members of the Executive Council bravely determined to borrow a further £200,000 to complete the purchase and redevelopment of Oak Tree Farm just outside Carlisle, formerly a small dairy farm, offered for sale by public auction by Smiths Gore and described as "an interesting traditional farmhouse, farm buildings and excellent arable and pasture land extending in total to 28.61 acres."

In the event, a long term supporter of the League, Lancelot MacGlasson died within a few days of that decision being taken, and his legacy subsequently obviated the need for borrowing.

The League had a new, larger and permanent home at last.

At Oak Tree Farm a modern surgery was desirable, office space essential, and a tea room and shop for visitors' use further necessities. Elsewhere, much more work was needed to customise the old buildings to accommodate a wide variety of equines, goats and sheep, plus the dogs, cats, wild animals, domesticated birds and wild, injured ones from the small animal unit, at Blackwell Road. Stabling, meeting rooms, kennels and a small parcel of three more acres of land were added, before Oak Tree Farm's official opening.

The move from Blackwell had a flavour of Noah's Ark about it, as the entire equine complement, together with a couple of goats and two sheep were moved in a single day. It was meticulously planned: in advance of the move stables were allocated, some for pairs of ponies, and others for single occupancy and the stables were even bedded down a day or so before, ready to receive the new inhabitants.

Les Moffat, a senior member of staff charged with overseeing the move, remembers it well:

"We made lists for everything which helped save time, and on the day it all fell into place nicely. The ponies were transported in a cattle wagon, by a fellow who had moved ponies across from the North East for us in the past, so he knew what he was doing. He spent the whole day running between Blackwell and Oak Tree Farm. All the ponies were haltered and loosely tied up – I think in total we moved about 30 equines, taking six or seven at a time on the wagon - and then when they arrived, they were stabled in their allocated accommodation. I seem to remember there was a media crew in amongst it all, with microphones and so on – I told them to stand well back from the ramp when we unloaded! The ponies all settled in really well, although of course, it was all new to them, the stables and the new pastures. We had to move all the hay and straw too, of course, though that was done a few days earlier, leaving just enough at Blackwell to last us through until we left. It was a long day, the day we moved, I remember that!"

Of course, if you chat to Outdoor Manager John Logan, he will tell you that he moved the entire refuge in his mini-van, and yes, we've all told him a million times about exaggerating…!

On Friday 25 June 1982 Her Royal Highness Princess Alexandra opened the farm as the new headquarters of the National Equine (and Smaller Animals) Defence League in a ceremony broadcast on BBC Radio Cumbria.

One thing remained unchanged, though: in 1983, 120 ponies still worked underground and retirees continued to be regularly accepted at Oak Tree Farm. Many of these ponies then pass into the care of Malcolm Kendall, who runs the League's Armathwaite establishment, not far from Wetheral (please note that this is not open to the public as it is on private land), and as we shall learn later, at the time of writing this history – mid 2008 - two deep-mine ponies, Gypsy and Scout, remain in the care of the League, having 'come up' from Ellington in 1994.

Contrary to popular perception, then, pit ponies are not a phenomenon that disappeared decades ago, although their care and welfare improved dramatically with time, largely due to the work of the League. Interestingly, elsewhere in Europe, ponies were used in the pits until just five years ago, the last ones to work underground being those at the Wieliczka Salt Mine, near Krakow in Poland.

Wasp, another former pit pony celebrated his 50th birthday in 1998, having enjoyed as many years in retirement as he had in work: not a bad aim for any human, never mind a pony. Although Wasp is unusual, many of the ponies enjoy life well into their 30's and often into their 40's too.

And does this sound familiar? "We have noted during the year an increase in the amount of verbal abuse directed towards our staff by some members of the public whose animals for one reason or another have come into our care. This is a matter that our Organising Secretary has felt obliged to discuss with the Police Authority. It seems to be symptomatic of the age in which we live…" That's from the annual Report of 1988, twenty years ago – there's nothing new under the sun, is there?

The New Millennium

The League picked its way carefully through the maze of the Foot and Mouth outbreak in 2001, refusing to give up its animals voluntarily although co-operating with MAFF/DEFRA as far as blood-testing of stock was concerned and calling throughout for a cohesive policy of vaccination. The League refused to accept that the slaughter of millions of healthy animals was either acceptable or justifiable, and it trod a delicate, but always principled, line through those difficult times.

The madness and mayhem of 2001 over, Organising Secretary Frank Tebbutt announced his intention of retiring in 2002, having worked for the League for 38 years, the first eight of those alongside the indefatigable Brisco, with whom he enjoyed a close bond. In 2002 a new kennel block was built, maintenance and improvement of the facilities at Oak Tree Farm being constantly necessary. As a permanent tribute to his dedication and hard work during his long service at the Refuge, the new kennel block was named The Frank Tebbut Kennels. In his stead, and with a new title, that of Director, Heather McLean was appointed to head up the League.

Changing technologies and regulations have necessitated changed procedures at the League. Horse Passports were introduced in 2004, the UK government having interpreted this European ruling in such a way that it required every equine to possess a passport. The idea was to ensure that no horses or ponies that had been administered particular drugs could enter the food chain, though there were certainly other, easier ways of ensuring this. Had microchipping or freeze-branding been allied to the passport system, it might have helped restore strayed or stolen animals to their rightful owners, but as it relies on an outdated system of identification, it has simply ended up as an

Alfred Brisco and friend

'Footloose and fancy free' at Longdales, August 21st 1969

Cleo and pups, born at the Refuge

Pony trussed and suspended underneath cage for lowering into the mine.

A working pit pony, picture taken in the 1970's.
Greatly improved working conditions and animal welfare are due in no small
measure to the ceaseless efforts of the League.

A new member of the Refuge staff undergoing telephony training

Malcolm Kendall, left, with his father, younger brother and a pit pony at Blackwell

Gypsy, whose retirement has been long and very happy.

A sign erected by the League, imploring carriage drivers to slacken the bearing and hame reins on steep inclines.

Lexie's colt foal, Leo. Leo and his mum, full name Do Blexa, were amongst the recent draft of ponies rescued in France, and saved from both slaughter and an atrocious journey to Italy.

One of the many free range cats at the Refuge

A young John Logan with an early dog warden van. This service (but not this van) is still operated by the Refuge.

expensive and rather pointless piece of bureaucratic nonsense, and yet another financial burden for a charity such as the League. Similarly, new cattle movement regulations have complicated things for the bovines, but again, working with the relevant agencies (and with a little help from our friends in places of influence!) such difficulties can be overcome.

Dogs and cats adopted through the Approved Homes Scheme are microchipped before they leave the Refuge – this means that if they stray, they can be scanned, traced back to the Refuge and then returned to their adoptive home safely. The League encourages microchipping of pets and offers this service at a very reasonable rate. Similarly, and in line with long-standing policy, male dogs are neutered before they leave and female ones either spayed before they go to their new adoptive home, or arrangements made at the time of adoption for that to be done: unwanted litters are to be avoided at all costs.

Figures from 2007, the most recent complete statistics available at the time of writing indicate that a total of 507 pets found new homes via the League: an astonishing figure. Oak Tree Farm's residents numbered 24 horses and ponies, 5 donkeys, 15 goats, 18 sheep, three cattle and 14 cats permanently resident. Up to 80 cats, 50 dogs, 30 rabbits, 25 ferrets and other small creatures – chinchillas, guinea pigs, and rats were waiting to find new owners. There's also a talking crow, who imitates dogs by barking convincingly, and telephones (attempts to change her ring-tone have been unsuccessful) and shouts 'hello' to passers-by (just be grateful she hasn't picked up anything more fruity in terms of language), countless other birds, wild and domestic, as well as several rather more exotic inhabitants.

Quite what Francis Cox would have made of a talking crow, one can only guess at…

2007 also saw the adoption of a new logo, reflecting the fact that locally, the National Equine (and smaller animals) Defence League, as it is properly known, is referred to as the Animals' Refuge. Sometimes, just the word "Wetheral" is enough to convey the meaning, but perhaps that would have been a step too far! The new logo is simple, effective, instantly recognisable; it appears on all headed notepaper, signs, and uniforms.

The Refuge, as a registered Charity, has a board of Trustees, who meet regularly to deal with policy and management issues, and of course, a Director, as previously mentioned. As we saw, in the early years, supporters included luminaries such as Keir Hardie, Winston Churchill and Jerome K Jerome; more recently Patrons have included David Bellamy, Katie Boyle and Chris Bonnington. All important people, but every bit as vital are those long-standing, devoted supporters of the work of the Refuge, as well as the army of staff and volunteers without whom it, quite simply, could not function effectively. If you visit Oak Tree Farm, you will see office and outside teams of staff wearing official Animals' Refuge T-shirts. They are ably assisted by an army of dedicated volunteers who also fundraise tirelessly and assist the staff with essential activities such as dog walking, and Cat Cuddling.

For many years the Refuge has been fortunate in having veterinary assistance from Craig Robinson and Partners, a long-established practice in Carlisle, and other experts are called on when necessary – blacksmiths, back men, horse dentists. Every year sees open days, dog shows, organised walks, fairs, and events, all of which make valuable contributions to financing ongoing work. There is a shop at Oak Tree Farm too, stocked with Christmas cards, books, bric-a-brac, and a great range of pet-related items - dog biscuits, cat collars, treats, beds... oh, and of course, doggy-poo bags.

For the past couple of decades, the League has operated a Dog Warden scheme on behalf of Carlisle City Council, taking in strays and caring for them until they have been claimed. If they are not claimed, the City Council gifts them to the Refuge, and then they can be rehomed. During 2007, some 471 stray dogs came into the Refuge; if not claimed within seven days, the dog becomes the property of the Refuge. At this point, it is assessed and if humanly possible, found a new home. The big advantage of adopting a stray from the Refuge, is that they will tell you everything they know about it: whether it is good with children, clean, walks well on a lead and so on; such a dog is less of an unknown quantity than one might have feared!

That said, there are, sadly, always a few dogs that cannot be rehomed: the seriously infirm, the dangerous – and in keeping with Alfred Brisco's belief that there were worse fates than a painless end, this is sometimes the most responsible and indeed, compassionate, course of action. Workaholics, too, can be difficult to rehome. Some springer spaniels are suitable as pets, but some are not: however, they make fantastic drug or explosive detection dogs and it's good to know that some former inmates are gainfully and extremely happily – Springers like nothing better than springing about and sniffing things – employed, and targeting dangerous crime.

One thing remains certain: any healthy animal has more than half a fighting chance once they pass through the gates of Oak Tree Farm. And that is far better odds than they had outside those gates.

Memories...

... Malcolm Kendall and Joan Mate, both long-standing employees, share their memories

Malcolm Kendall, whose association with the Animals' Refuge ponies stretches back into his early childhood, looks back over the past fifty years.

It must be difficult for Malcolm Kendall to remember a time when the Animals' Refuge didn't feature prominently in his life.

Born and brought up at Armathwaite, Malcolm now lives in the house where his grandmother once lived, and it was through her friendship with the redoubtable Alfred Brisco that ponies first came to Armathwaite in the fifties. Malcolm explains: "they were great friends, Mr Brisco and my grandmother, both, I believe, lay-preachers. There would have been about ten acres here in those days, and like everybody else back then, we kept a house cow and a pig, but all our pets – guinea pigs and rabbits came from Alf. There was spare grazing here, but little at Durdar, so some of the pit ponies came out here for a bit of good grass." They must have thought they had landed in Paradise: after twenty years down the pits, the freedom and lushness of Armathwaite's pasture must have been, to say the least, a welcome change.

Malcolm's first pony, a little bay mare called Sally, came from Alf, in 1957. David, a skewbald Shetland, followed. Both of them worked, Malcolm remembers, pulling a little cart. The ponies at Durdar at this time were housed in redundant railway wagons - less than ideal, perhaps by modern day standards, but perfectly adequate, while at Armathwaite three small stables were constructed. Then Howard Bliss provided the money for some 'proper' stables and twelve were built, using mainly second hand materials - corrugated Asbestos roofs, reclaimed floorboards and, as an imaginative addition, sleepered walkways outside, each one partitioned from its neighbour to allow the ponies fresh air, essential as the ponies were kept inside during winter.

It was all very different fifty years ago, Malcolm recalls : " the League survived on a hand-to-mouth basis. There were no post and rail fenced paddocks, no purpose-built stables, nothing like that. And you should have seen the first trailer we had: it was home made, a recycled chassis and bits of tin, bent and welded here and there – no mudguards or anything, and we pulled it with an old Cortina. It was roadworthy enough for those times, but of course, now we have a Land Rover and proper horse trailer to transport everything."

Later on, another twelve boxes that had been at Durdar were dismantled and reconstructed at Armathwaite, and pony numbers – all of them from the pits – gradually increased from the original pair in 1957 to 32 in 1967. Malcolm remembers that as a boy still at school, he helped out in the stables and two further men, one of them a tenant of the Kendall's, also looked after the ponies. "I think I just had more interest in ponies than my brothers – and later on I inherited Great Uncle Jim's kit. Great Uncle Jim," he adds, "was the Ainstable blacksmith," and therefore has a bit to answer for, since Malcolm ended up being responsible for trimming the hooves of all the equines in the care of the League for a number of years. These days, he just does the ones at Armathwaite and a blacksmith visits Wetheral to attend to the residents there.

Malcolm himself was formally employed by the League in 1970 and remains on the staff to this day, caring for the many ponies – the number is fairly steady at around thirty – at Armathwaite, where he now has 16 hectares of land. One pony he remembers with particular affection is another Sally, whose pictures tell a sad story: the victim of a family split, vets held little hope for her survival when she arrived at Armathwaite. A sling was rigged up out of hessian as she was too weak to stand, and slowly but surely, the mare recovered. The picture of a confident and pretty little grey mare in Malcolm's family photograph album betrays no clues as to her inauspicious start, but speaks volumes about the care she received. Another character was the racehorse, Chateau Royale – Roy – who won the Caesarawitch (a long distance flat race) but ended his days in leisurely retirement in the Eden Valley; Roy, black, elegant and really rather regal, grazing amongst pit ponies, in the fields owned by the League near Ainstable Church, was a vision to gladden the coldest heart. Another was old Ruler, a pit pony who lived well into his forties and was much missed as a real little character; in fact, most of the pit ponies lived into their thirties and several, like Ruler, into their forties.

These days, there are just two pit ponies left, from the deep mines, Gypsy and Scout, who came to the Refuge in 1994 from Ellington Combine, the last mine in England to use ponies underground. Malcolm recalls that Gypsy and Scout, who worked 12 miles out under the sea, on retirement both needed power tool work - the equine equivalent of root canal treatment - on their ageing teeth. They are still very much alive, and sometimes even kicking at the time of writing.

Although there will be no pit ponies in the future, equines still come to the League, and from many disparate sources: one pony was abandoned tied to a post, others have been found wandering in Carlisle, or roaming on the A6, and then there are those who are simply given to the League by owners who have died or are unable to continue caring for their animals.

Before wholesale pit closures, another of Malcolm's tasks was to collect the ponies from the mines, using that proper horse trailer naturally, and transport them to their new lives of ease. "What was really odd about this, was that I had to collect them from Stores, because that is what they were regarded as within the mining industry - a 'Store' item. Officially they were supposed to work an eight-hour shift and they did not come up to the surface during the course of their working lives. When they did, it was after twenty years of work below ground. It was a hard life for them, by any standards." Contrary to popular myth, Malcolm says that the ponies experienced few problems with their sight, but respiratory difficulties, lameness and injuries were common.

Pit ponies were trained to voice commands and developed a close bond with their handlers who were called horsekeepers; there were two horsekeepers on each shift and Malcolm remembers many of the miners being devoted to the ponies with whom they shared their working lives – thankfully, much had changed since those early days of 1909, when the ponies were often callously treated by their handlers. "The tales some of those old miners told, when I met them. The thing was, the ponies were such characters too - one, I remember, used to ride on the conveyor with his horsekeeper at the end of each shift – imagine that! And if a ton of feed was loaded on to a conveyor, but the time it reached its destination, there was a lot less than that, the miners having pinched extra rations for their favourite ponies. These big hard men, lots of them were soft as butter where their ponies were concerned."

There was a suggestion that it would be a good idea to replace two of the 24 boxes a year, Malcolm recalls, but this was really not practical and in 1982, a new range of stabling was built at Armathwaite. A second building, roughly approximate to an American barn, incorporating all the lessons from the first construction was added later and the ponies live in some considerable comfort here. The advantage of the 'barn' system for the ponies is that they can see one another, and for the humans it is that they can work in the dry! Although Malcolm mainly works at Armathwaite, he is a regular visitor to Wetheral, a matter of a few miles away, and remembers the early days of the League's acquisition of Oak Tree Farm. "There were nettles waist high in places, and of course, none of the purpose built stabling that there is now. The changes have been enormous."

Malcolm remembers that Alfred Brisco used to go to horse sales, on a constant mission to educate people about animal welfare. These days, such sales are far better policed than they were then, and the cruelty once seen at the sales is no longer commonplace. Malcolm too, visits sales and occasionally buys ponies, but this is a difficult area. If charities such as the League were to buy large numbers of ponies, an unrealistic market would quickly establish, and in the long term this would be completely counter-productive.

Malcolm's work nowadays involves the day-to-day care of the League's herd of equines at Armathwaite – feeding, foot-trimming and so on, management of their grazing and the field shelters that are in every field for use during inclement weather. There is hay to make on site in summer, and continuous maintenance of stabling and facilities. Additionally, Malcolm will often be required to visit prospective loan homes to ensure that the adopters have sufficient knowledge and facilities to care for the League's animals properly and transport the ponies between grazing stints when the need arises, although "we don't shift them about nearly as much these days. In the past, we used to swap the ponies between Carlisle and Armathwaite, but since Oak Tree Farm was acquired, this is no longer necessary." Every effort is made to keep the ponies in as natural a state as possible; they are turned out during the summer, either on land owned by the League in Ainstable or on Malcolm's own pasture.

Horses are naturally sociable animals, never happy alone, and noticeably, they form into small herds in the fields. During winter they turned out as much as the Cumbrian weather permits, and are stabled at night; they have plentiful rations of good hay, and a diet based on soaked sugar beet, partly because, Malcolm points out, this is succulent and soft and therefore very suitable for elderly ponies whose teeth can cause them discomfort.

Just like us, ponies suffer with more health problems as they get older and they are by no means confined to their teeth. Sweet-itch, a summertime skin allergy is one of the most unpleasant and causes the sufferer terrible irritation and discomfort; modern solutions include topical skin treatments, special rugs, and restricting turn-out time to avoid the midges that cause the condition. Laminitis is another horror: caused by the succulent summer grass – basically eating too much rich food, and in the case of Shetlands and other native or small ponies, too much is not really very much at all if they are susceptible - the inside of the hoof becomes inflamed, and since it is encased in a solid block – the hoof – the laminae cannot swell, and pain ensues. The only real treatment for laminitis is to remove the sufferer to a bare patch of land and feed small quantities of hay rather than grass. Dealing with such ailments is not just enormously time consuming, it also requires compassion, something so often lacking in the earlier lives of animals that end up in the League's care.

Malcolm is now in his mid-fifties. As a boy, he was willing child-labour, and has worked for the League his entire adult life. He has seen, and indeed been part of, major changes in the League's history, but one thing has remained constant: the most wonderful care given to every pony at Armathwaite.

Joan Mate, like Malcolm, has enjoyed an association with the League that goes back to her youth. Here, she too looks back on the changes she has witnessed

There is no feminine version of the phrase "man and boy" so often trotted out to describe a man's lifetime service to one employer. If there were, it should be used now, to refer to Joan Mate, who retired in 2008, after quite literally, a lifetime's service to the Animals' Refuge.

Whilst still a teenager, and when the Refuge was established at Blackwell Road, Currock, just down the road from the Home of Rest for Horses, Joan would help out in school holidays and at weekends. She remembers Alfred - Mr Brisco - well, from that time. "He didn't suffer fools," she says, adding with a twinkle, "and he wasn't at all pleasant to anyone who harmed animals. He was a most compassionate man, kind and generous – he would take me, another girl who also helped out, and his secretary out for trips in the van to the Lake District. We'd often end up at some nice hostelry." Of course, Joan and I smile at the thought – given our modern day cynicism - at the raised eyebrows and disapproving looks that the spectacle of an elderly gentleman, accompanied by three pretty young girls might attract now. Happily, those were more innocent times. And it's probably fair to say that Alfred himself would have had to modify his own management style, and – heaven preserve us – his People Skills, in twenty first Century Britain. That said, it's not to suggest that he was wrong in any way!

After a secretarial course at college, Joan joined the Refuge on a full time basis, working as Mr Brisco's secretary and she also helped out on outside duties. The actual work of the Refuge was much the same as it is now, meeting the same need, taking in animals that people could no longer keep, for whatever reason, and finding them suitable new homes, and Joan recalls even more unwanted puppies and kittens then than now. Alfred Brisco was keen that people should be educated in responsible animal ownership, part of which focused on the need to neuter dogs and cats in order to prevent unwanted pregnancies: he promoted, essentially, family planning for pets. Joan also remembers Alfred Brisco's firmly held belief that there were worse fates for an animal than a humane death. He had to put many animals to sleep, never something undertaken lightly, and never, Joan asserts something one ever becomes inured to. But it is sometimes the most responsible course of action, in the case, for example of a dog unsafe to rehome, and unavoidable in the case of an animal for whom quality of life has evaporated in lieu of unremitting pain.

Alfred Brisco worked up until his death for the cause that became his life's work: animal welfare. He never properly retired, and was survived by several years by his wife Peggy. They had no children.

For Joan herself, marriage and family intervened, and she stopped working for a time, rejoining the staff later on a part time basis. "Of course, in those days," she recalls, "you had to claw your way back up the promotion ladder! There was no maternity leave or anything like that. Shorthand was essential for a secretary, and we just had a manual typewriter and a telephone in the office then." By the time the Refuge relocated to Oak Tree Farm in 1981, Frank Tebbutt had become Organising Secretary, with Joan as his secretary, and the staff, both office personnel and outside staff, had increased dramatically to care for the numerous horses, ponies, dogs, cats and various other creatures feathered, furred or finned now resident at Wetheral. "We were still plinking away on manual typewriters, two of them now," Joan smiles. The first computer arrived in 1987, and, in order to learn how to tame the beast, Joan went off on a computer course.

Nowadays, over 500 dogs a year pass through the Refuge, many of them as a result of the Dog Warden work that the Refuge undertakes on behalf of Carlisle City Council. As well as dogs, and the ponies who really started the whole thing off, there are cats, rodents, reptiles, ferrets, goats, sheep cattle at the Refuge… the list is endless. Just as diverse are the humans Joan has encountered over the years. "Some of them," she says crisply, "don't deserve their animals' loyalty at all. They get them too easily, and cast them aside just as carelessly."

Joan's retirement will, of course, include spending more time with her family, her dog and four cats, and lots of dog walking, but it is inconceivable that she will sever her ties with the Refuge. "Oh no," she says, "I hope I'll still just walk in the office and say, 'I'm back' every now and then!"
And she does.

A Day at the Refuge

We are often asked what it is like to work at the Refuge, and what a normal day is like. Every day is different, and unexpected things often happen. If we ever find out what normal is, we will let you know. An average day might go a bit like this:-

8. 15 am:
The Outdoor Team (who take care of the animals) arrive to start work at 8.30 am. As they walk down the drive, they are greeted by the goats in the front field and waylaid by outdoor cats Arthur and Oscar, who are tapping their watches and wanting to know when someone will oblige with the tin opener and the cat food. Everyone gathers in the Kitchen, where those who have been off can look back on the Daybook (an informal diary) to find out what has been happening. The Daybook is an important tool - used to make sure everyone is made aware of any animals that are off-colour or on treatment; or to give general reminders for planned activities.

8.30 am:
Outdoor Manager John Logan allocates duties for the morning. On his days off, this is done by either of the Team Leaders, Julie Hardie or Ian Slater. Today, Julie is on kitchen duty, while Janet Meakins looks after the Tebbutt Kennel, where stray dogs are housed, and Jackie Ruddick takes care of the Margaret Heatley Kennel. Sue Wright is on the Cattery, while Matthew McCowan covers the top ponies. This doesn't just involve looking after horses, as it includes any animals in the admissions unit and Orchard Yard, the goats in the orchard, and the birds and fish in the office reception area. Andrew Fisher looks after the stable yard. Later, he is assigned to help Nigel the Handyman with some fence repairs in the Oaks field. Ian Slater will take care of

the ponies and cattle in the fields, and Caroline Gemmell is on van driving duties. Jamie Wright is on rabbits, while Sarah is helping Julie in the kitchen. Sarah will also look after the puppies and cats, some of the small animals and the dogs in the Cowx unit. Gillian Dixon, Corrinne Paton, Lesley McLean Rachael Hope, Carol Fisher and Ellen Wilson are all on days off today. They were all working over the weekend, but will return later in the week.

8.45 am:
With work underway outside, Office Manager Joan Mate opens the office in readiness for the official start at 9 am, when the Refuge opens to visitors. As the rest of the office team arrive, the toilets and front doors are unlocked, computers are switched on and the night-time answering machine is turned off as the switchboard reopens. John has already taken the radios for the outdoor team. Joan calls Matthew to find out if any stray dogs have been lodged in the holding kennel overnight. We have an arrangement with the Police that any strays picked up out with working hours will be brought to the Refuge and put into a kennel (already set up with food, water and bedding), and the relevant form filled in showing where and when the animal was found. Matthew reports that a small brindle and white Staffordshire bull terrier bitch was brought in at midnight. He will bring the paperwork over in a few minutes.

9 am:
In the office, the phones begin to ring. A lady reports her missing cat. Val notes the details in the lost cat register, and advises on steps the owner can take to help find her pet.

Today, Julie is on Kitchen duties. This is a vital role, as it involves co-ordinating communication between the office and the rest of the Outdoor Team. She will also carry out interviews, provide information on animals which people are considering adopting, prepare food for cats and puppies, and administer medication to any animals that are on treatment from the Vet. Sarah will assist her today. She is being trained to interview people wanting to adopt, and needs to understand Kitchen duties.

10 am:

Tea break for the Outdoor Team. Everyone gathers in the food preparation room for coffee, biscuits and gossip. The cats grudgingly move over to allow their human companions a few inches of sofa. Outdoor cat Josephine settles on Jamie's lap and starts purring. If he doesn't give her enough attention she will swipe him with her claws. Preferring not to bleed, he tactfully lifts her onto a cushion. She stalks off in a huff, but will be back soon to find another victim.

In the office, the owner of the dog brought in from the Police last night has phoned. He's been frantically looking for his pet and is very grateful to know she is safe. Nettie tells him about the Council charge and our boarding fee. He will come to claim his dog as soon as he can. Not all dog owners are so pleasant to deal with. A small minority of people claiming lost pets are rude and aggressive, especially when they hear about the penalty the Council charge for allowing a dog to stray.

Val is making an appointment for a family who want to adopt a rabbit. They will be here at 2 pm. Joan is arranging appointment times for three bitches that were adopted a few months ago to be neutered through our vets. With strays, it isn't always easy to know if a bitch has been spayed. The safest time to neuter is at the mid-point between two seasons, so people who adopt bitches are asked to let us know as soon as their new pet comes into season. Joan then calculates the safest time to operate, and schedules their appointment accordingly.

10.30 am:

Tracey breaks off from typing up the minutes of a recent meeting and makes coffee for everyone in the office. Although this is a break, work can't stop completely. If the phone rings or a customer needs help then the office staff will deal with it.

In the stable yard, Andrew sings as he mucks out the goat stable. His music-loving colleagues cover their ears and beg until he agrees to stop. Janet's dog, Blue, is disappointed - he had been planning to join in at the chorus. John is interviewing a couple who want to adopt a small dog. Sarah has almost finished cleaning out the ferrets. Now she has to work out how to get out of the enclosure without the ferrets following. They've had fun chasing the brush and exploring the bucket, and see no reason why such an exciting playmate should leave. She leaps nimbly over the inner gate and moves on to her next task.

11 am:

Val goes through the paperwork with the owner of the Staffie cross. Matthew brings the little bitch over from the holding kennel and dog and owner share a very happy reunion. Val give advice on the need for the dog to have a tag on her collar with the owner's address and phone number, (but crucially, not the dog's name). She also suggests microchipping. The owner decides to go ahead, and Val calls Julie to come up and implant the chip right away.

12 pm:

The first lunch breaks begin for the Office. Joan goes first. Nettie will take her break when Joan returns, and Val will follow Nettie. If there are more staff on duty, breaks will overlap.

<u>12.30 pm:</u>
All the part time Animal Welfare Workers on duty this morning finish for the day. The Outdoor Team take their break starting any time between 12.30 and 1.30 pm, depending on workload. Julie has the radio, and will deal with anything that comes up over lunch time.

<u>1.15 pm:</u>
In the office, Heather prepares cash and cheques, ready to take to the bank. Tracey is finished with paid work for the day, and goes home to bravely tackle a large basket of ironing.

<u>1.30 pm:</u>
Everyone is hard at work. Matthew is in charge of recycling. Every few days he goes round the various recycling bins gathering plastic, paper, card and tins and taking them to the central collection point. Today, he has gathered enough plastic and tin to fill the containers, so he asks Val to arrange an uplift from the recycling company. Jackie is going out in the van. She is the Dog Warden for the afternoon, and is going to collect a stray dog at an address in Harraby. The householder has caught a Labrador that was wandering in the street. While she is out, Jackie will patrol other parts of the city, looking for unattended dogs. She also has a short shopping list - Julie needs some chicken for a poorly cat, and the rabbits and guinea pigs need fresh vegetables. Joan gives her the address of the person who has found the Labrador, and asks her to sign a petty cash voucher before giving her money for the animal food.

The family who want a rabbit have arrived for the two o'clock appointment. Julie will interview them and if all is well will show them the rabbits. John is off to carry out some follow-up visits around Keswick and Cockermouth. He will be out for the rest of the afternoon.

Sue is in the cattery. There are five cats due to be wormed, and one semi-longhair that would benefit from grooming. Janet is spending time with an unclaimed dog. It is a collie cross which she wants to get to know before she can assess his suitability for rehoming. Initial signs are good. He sits, stays and gives paws, plays happily and doesn't show any signs of aggression. While he is a little boisterous, he seems happy about the other dogs being around, and ignores Inca the cat as he stalks past on the other side of the fence. Sarah and Jackie have already made favourable reports, and if he doesn't give Janet any cause for concern he will be moved to the Margaret Heatley Kennel and put up for adoption.

Sue Solomon signs in at the office. She is a regular Dog Walker, and will spend quality time in the K9 Playpen with some of the residents.

2 pm:
Julie and Janet start to feed the dogs. They are excited and noisy. All are keen to eat. Janet will be back later to clear away and wash the dishes.

2.20 pm:
A couple who booked a cat two days ago come to collect their new pet. Julie checks the cat over and microchips her. On the rehoming information form, she notes down when the cat was vaccinated and wormed (and the drugs used), and information on any veterinary treatment it has had recently. Then she calls the office on the radio give them details of the cat - her tag number and the date that she came in from a home. Val will complete the paperwork, and the adoption agreement. By the time the cat and her people arrive in reception, she will have the vaccination certificate looked out and information. She will go over the agreement with them, and give advice on settling

the cat into its new home. If there are any veterinary problems in the first few days, she advises them to contact the Refuge so that we can arrange appropriate treatment. It is not uncommon for small ailments to come to light with all the excitement and upheaval of going into a new home. The agreement signed, the cat and her new family set off to start their lives together. Hopefully, this will be a relationship that endures for many years.

Matthew has finished his recycling collection, and is trimming the goats' hooves. Andrew and Nigel are repairing a fence in the Oaks field, while Ian is working with Blitz and Bandit to socialise them. He is getting them used to having their feet lifted, and will do some training on walking on a halter. This is vital early education, which will help them develop into well-mannered ponies.

3.30 pm:
Jackie returns. The stray dog had been claimed by its owners before she arrived at the finder's house. However, she has picked up a small Jack Russell dog from outside a Primary School where it was running in and out of the playground. Jackie gives a detailed description of the dog to Joan, and notes down the place and time it was collected, and the time of admission to the Refuge. This is all information that the City Council require.

The family that Julie interviewed have come to the office to book a home visit. They already have one rabbit, which needs a companion. Nettie takes the details. Jackie will visit later in the week to see the hutch where the rabbits will be kept. Janet is in the interview room, writing up an assessment sheet for the collie cross. He will be vaccinated when the vet comes in tomorrow, and will go up for adoption.

<u>4 pm:</u>

Janet and Julie go to settle the dogs, while Sue has a final check round the cattery before locking up for the night. Ian is in the fields for a last look at the ponies. In the office, Nettie locks up reception, while Val closes the tills and cashes up. Everything balances, so she completes her records and locks the safe. Joan is recording holiday applications, and Heather is working on the bank reconciliation for last month.

<u>4.45 pm:</u>

Julie brings the radio back to the office for charging. She has a short chat with Joan about a bitch and two tom cats that she wants to have neutered next Monday. Joan will contact the Vet tomorrow, and make the arrangements.

<u>5 pm:</u>

The end of a long day. All of the staff go home. The dogs and cats are settled for the night. For the larger animals, there is still time to graze in the late evening sunshine. Heather and her family will enjoy a walk round before bed time to fuss the horses, goats and any of the outdoor cats who happen to be around. John also lives on site, and will probably have a walk out round the farm later. With work over, it is a very pleasant way to end the day.

Full Circle...

Mindful of the approaching Centenary, and wishing to reignite debate and awareness about transport of equines, something of long-standing concern to the League throughout its history, in late 2008, a group of equines were brought to the Refuge, from Europe. Had this little band - four pregnant Pottok mares with their foals at foot, a Breton filly, a Comtois gelding and an Ardennes colt - have survived a gruelling three day journey from France to Italy, their destination was an Italian slaughterhouse.

Whilst the League does not have an issue with horse meat if the trade is carried out under humane conditions, it does object strongly to horses being moved around Europe in appalling conditions. It is, shockingly, still legal for horses to travel in lorries for up to 24 hours without food, water or rest. Worse, even these rules are often breached, and many animals die in squalid misery before they reach their destination. The League urges action on this, obviously.

These ponies are all settled in the Cumbrian countryside, being handled and cared for at the Refuge. Eventually, those suitable will be adopted by caring and experienced homes where they can enjoy a useful, happy life and others will remain at Oak Tree Farm.

And finally...

Many thousands of animals and visitors have passed through the gates of Oak Tree Farm, since the League moved its operations there and it is worth speculating on what Francis Cox and Alfred Brisco might make of the Refuge now, with its office buzzing with computers, its numerous staff, the carefully constructed shelters, buildings, fenced paddocks, the fantastic comfort of the modern cattery and more unfamiliar innovations such as microchipping, passporting and so on. One hopes that the dismay they might feel that such a need still exists, and on such a scale in times of relative affluence, might be tempered with enormous pride at the work that dedicated staff and volunteers, several of them of many, many years standing, continue to perform to improve the lot of animals of all kinds.

After all, much has changed, but the principles that underpin the work of the League remain exactly the same as they were in 1909: to improve the lot of animals and to educate the public about their care and welfare.

To find out more about the work of the Refuge, making a donation towards its continuing work, adopting or sponsoring an animal, volunteering to help at the Refuge in some capacity, or dog walking, visit www.animalrefuge.co.uk

Or contact the office at
The Animals Refuge
Oak Tree Farm
Wetheral Shields
Carlisle
CA4 8JA

Tel: 01228 560082
Fax: 01228 560985

About the Author

Jackie has researched and written this brief history as a small thank you to the Refuge for Katie Morag, who she describes as probably the most rewarding dog she has ever owned.

Jackie Moffat is a columnist, writer and author of the bestselling *The Funny Farm* and *Sheepwrecked.* She lives in the Eden Valley with her husband, a flock of Manx Loaghtan sheep, a couple of Fell ponies and the incomparable, inimitable Katie Morag, a lurcher whose previous address was Oak Tree Farm.